KING ST.

Set Two
BOOK I

New Neighbours

New Neighbours
King Street: Readers Set Two - Book 1
Copyright © Iris Nunn 2014

Text: Iris Nunn
Editor: June Lewis
Illustrations: Pip Jones and Marta Kwasniewska

Published in 2014 by Gatehouse Media Limited

ISBN: 978-1-84231-116-5

British Library Cataloguing-in-Publication Data:
A catalogue record for this book is available from the British Library

The doorbell rang
at number sixteen.
Jane opened the door.

"Hello, I am Bill Smith
from next door."

"Pleased to meet you,"
said Jane. "Come in!"

Bill and his wife, Ann,
have just moved
into number fourteen.

They have a baby.
Tom is three months old.

Bill wanted to find out
about the nearest doctor.

"I like this street.
The people are very friendly."

"We like to help,"
said Jane.

Bill is a bus driver.
He works for Kingsmead Transport.

Ann stays at home
and looks after the baby.

She used to work
in a hospital.

"Tell Ann to come round
with the baby.
The twins would like to play
with him."

"Yes, Ann would like that too," said Bill.

Bill was glad they had moved
to King Street.